Cornerstones of Freedom

The Santa Fe Trail

JUDY ALTER

CHILDREN'S PRESS®
A Division of Grolier Publishing
New York • London • Hong Kong • Sydney
Danbury, Connecticut

Visit Children's Press on the Internet at:
http://publishing.grolier.com

Library of Congress Cataloging-in-Publication Data

Alter, Judy, 1938–
    The Santa Fe Trail / Judy Alter.
      p. cm.—(Cornerstones of freedom)
    Includes index.
    Summary: Presents a history of the trail that became an important
commercial route to the southwestern United States during the 1800s.
    ISBN: 0-516-21145-5 (lib. bdg.)   0-516-26396-X (pbk.)
    1. Santa Fe Trail—History—Juvenile literature. [1. Santa Fe Trail—
History.] I. Title. II. Series.
F786.A52   1998
978—dc21
                                                    97-32710
                                                        CIP
                                                        AC

Americans have always looked to the West for opportunity and a better life. For settlers in the original thirteen colonies, bounded on the east by the Atlantic Ocean, west was the only direction they could go to seek more land and more freedom. By the early 1800s, settlers and adventurers had crossed the Allegheny Mountains and pushed their way west to the Mississippi River. But nobody knew much about the land beyond the Mississippi.

The first European settlers to what became the United States arrived on its eastern shores. The settlers' desire for more land and greater opportunities drove them west.

Americans knew that the Southwest was Spanish territory. The Spanish guarded their land carefully because they did not trust the United States government. They didn't want Americans to move onto their land. But the Spanish secretiveness only fired American imaginations. Many Americans believed the Spanish were hiding great riches in the Southwest.

The Santa Fe Trail, in use from 1822 to 1879, opened the Southwest to American trade. It also provided fortunes for many American traders.

By the 1800s, rumors of treasure in the Spanish Southwest had spread throughout the young United States.

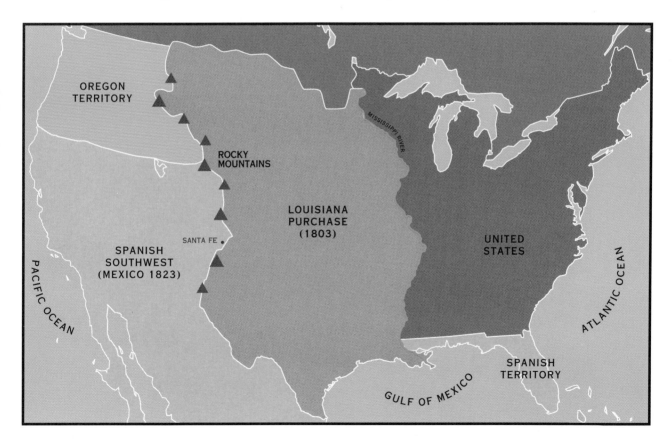

The Oregon Trail was traveled by pioneers seeking new homesteads. The Chisholm Trail was used for cattle drives. Cowboys took the animals north from Texas to the railroad in Abilene, Kansas, for shipping to markets in the East. The Santa Fe Trail was a commercial trail created for traders to take goods to Santa Fe, in present-day New Mexico. There, the traders would sell them and return home with saddle-bags full of gold or silver. Like most trails, the Santa Fe Trail was not a clearly defined path, but a series of different trails. These trails sometimes went in different directions, and at other times, they crossed each other. By the middle of the 1800s, deep ruts left by wagon wheels marked many places along the trail. Wagonners had only to follow the ruts in order to stay on the trail. Today, the trail is difficult to find in most spots, although in some places it is easier to see from a low-flying airplane.

Wagon wheels made deep, narrow tracks, called ruts, along the Santa Fe Trail. Although in most places the ruts are overgrown with grass, traces of the trail can still be seen.

The Santa Fe Trail covers almost 1,000 miles (1,610 kilometers) across the Great Plains to the Rocky Mountains. Today, you can travel it in one and a half days by automobile, or two hours by airplane. In the first years the trail was open, the journey took several months and involved hardship, danger, and sometimes death.

The first American to explore the path to Santa Fe was Lieutenant Zebulon Pike. In 1806, he was only twenty-seven years old when the U.S. Army sent him across the Great Plains and the Rocky Mountains to discover the mysteries of the Spanish Southwest. He took only twenty men with him, including a civilian named John Robinson. The story was told that Robinson was trying to recover goods that had been stolen from him by a man who had disappeared into the Southwest. But it is possible that Robinson was a spy. Pike and his army troop could not legally march into New Mexico because it was Spanish territory. Robinson, however, was allowed to enter New Mexico because he was a civilian. This may explain why he was part of a military mission.

Pike organized his expedition in St. Louis, Missouri. Unknown to him, Spanish spies were watching. Pike and his men traveled by keelboat up the Missouri River from St. Louis to a point about where Kansas City, Missouri, is today. From there, they went by horseback.

Zebulon Pike

Only three years earlier, in 1803, the Louisiana Purchase had doubled the size of the United States. The U.S. government, led by President Thomas Jefferson, bought the land from France for $11 million. The Purchase included all of the land between the Mississippi River and the Rocky Mountains, from the Gulf of Mexico to Canada. The amount of land included in the Purchase totaled about 800,000 square miles (1 million square km). The American government was anxious to explore its new territory. In 1804, the Lewis and Clark expedition was sent across the northern edge of the Purchase from St. Louis, Missouri, to the Pacific Ocean near present-day Astoria, Oregon. In 1805, Zebulon Pike had gone northward to the source of the Mississippi River.

Pike led nineteen men and one civilian across the Rocky Mountains toward the Spanish Southwest.

Now, as Pike set out once again, this time to explore the Southwest, one of his assignments was to visit American-Indian tribes. He was to make treaties between them and the United States government. One tribe, the Pawnee, warned Pike that a Spanish force of six hundred men was looking for his troops and had captured American traders. Pike refused to turn back to St. Louis. However, visiting with each tribe made the expedition's progress slow. Pike's party had left St. Louis in the spring of 1806, but they did not reach the foothills of the Colorado Rockies until late November.

The Pawnee lived on the prairies in the area from present-day Nebraska to New Mexico.

In Colorado, Pike came upon a great round mountain peak. He was unsuccessful in his attempt to climb it, but today it is known as Pike's Peak. It is one of the best-known mountains in the United States. The encounter with the mountain was the only highlight in an otherwise grim journey. The expedition's packhorses fell off a cliff. The soldiers lost their compass in the accident, so they had no way of knowing which direction to take. They had neither the appropriate clothing, nor enough food, to survive the harsh weather brought on by frigid mountain temperatures. But Pike would not give up.

Pike's Peak is 14,110 feet (4,300 meters) high.

When Pike and his men finally reached a tributary of the Rio Grande in present-day Colorado, they built a log fort. In February 1807, John Robinson left the fort and headed for Santa Fe.

Spanish troops soon arrived at Pike's fort. Robinson had reached Santa Fe, and the troops had followed his tracks back to Pike's party. Pike was forced to go to Santa Fe under guard. He refused the demand that he and his men give up their weapons. It would have disgraced him to enter Santa Fe as an unarmed soldier.

The Spanish troops reached Santa Fe with Pike and his soldiers on March 3, 1807. Expecting to see the treasures of the Southwest, Pike was disappointed. He found a small, shabby town with only a few adobe stores and houses. The narrow streets were crowded with donkeys that

In the early 1800s, Santa Fe, New Mexico, was a small town without the riches that Pike hoped to find.

the citizens rode, as well as two-wheeled oxcarts that were used for transporting goods.

The finest building in Santa Fe was the Governor's Palace on the Plaza. It had white-washed walls and skin rugs on its floors, and the interior was filled with massive hand-carved furniture and golden decorative pieces, such as candlesticks, that had probably been imported from Spain. These riches had likely been brought some 2,000 miles (3,000 km) by cart or pack mule up the Santa Fe Trail from Old Mexico (the present-day country of Mexico). Most of the goods the Santa Fe residents needed—clothing, furniture, cooking utensils, reading materials, and more—were brought the same way. It was, however, expensive to transport these goods so far under difficult conditions. As a result, everything cost more in Santa Fe than it did in either Old Mexico or St. Louis—facts Pike recorded in his journal.

Because the Spanish governor of New Mexico suspected that Pike and his men were spies, they were sent to the province of Chihuahua, in Old Mexico. After questioning, they were released and returned to the United States. Pike never returned to the Southwest. He died six years later fighting the British in the War of 1812. His journals were made public, however, and St. Louis merchants soon believed that there was a new market for their trade goods in Santa Fe.

In the years following Pike's expedition, several groups of traders set out on his trail. They were arrested by the Spanish, and their goods were taken. Two trappers, Jules DeMun and Auguste Chouteau, lost nearly $30,000 worth of skins that they had spent two years trapping. After this incident, traders and trappers avoided the Spanish.

William Becknell is credited with opening the Santa Fe Trail. In 1822, he led a small party of five men to Santa Fe from Franklin, Missouri. After Becknell's journey, Franklin was the starting point of the Santa Fe Trail until 1828, when a flood destroyed the town. (Independence, Missouri, then became the starting point.)

The trail Becknell followed became known as the Mountain Route. From Franklin, it went west to the Kansas border. Just over the border, beyond Olathe, Kansas, the Oregon Trail would in later

The Santa Fe Trail wound for 780 miles (1,260 kilometers), from Missouri to Santa Fe.

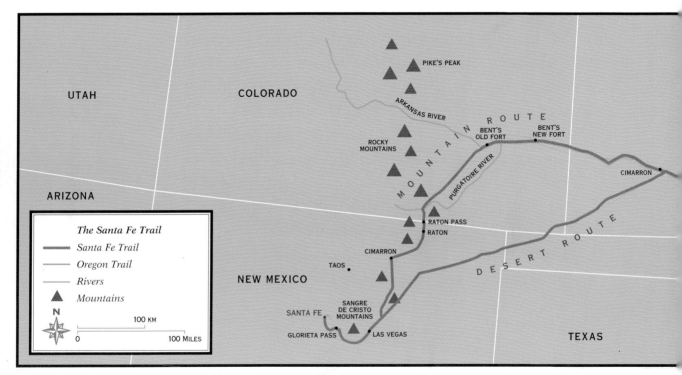

The Santa Fe Trail

— Santa Fe Trail
— Oregon Trail
— Rivers
▲ Mountains

N

100 KM

0   100 MILES

UTAH

COLORADO

PIKE'S PEAK

ARKANSAS RIVER

M O U N T A I N   R O U T E

BENT'S OLD FORT   BENT'S NEW FORT

ROCKY MOUNTAINS

PURGATOIRE RIVER

CIMARRON

ARIZONA

RATON PASS
RATON

CIMARRON

D E S E R T   R O U T E

TAOS

NEW MEXICO

SANGRE DE CRISTO MOUNTAINS

SANTA FE

GLORIETA PASS   LAS VEGAS

TEXAS

years fork to the north, taking settlers to the Pacific Northwest. But the Santa Fe Trail continued straight west across the grasslands of Kansas. In the early days, there were clumps of trees along the creeks and rivers, but over the years traders cut down almost all of the trees for firewood. For many easterners, accustomed to land covered with trees, the vast, open space was frightening.

Travelers on the trail next stopped at what later became Council Grove, Kansas, where water, wood, and grass were plentiful. There, teamsters (people who drove wagons loaded with goods) prepared for the difficult journey ahead. Lone teamsters would often wait until several more had gathered so they could make the dangerous trip together. Council Grove was considered the gateway to the Plains. Today, the town is known as "The Rendezvous of the Santa Fe Trail."

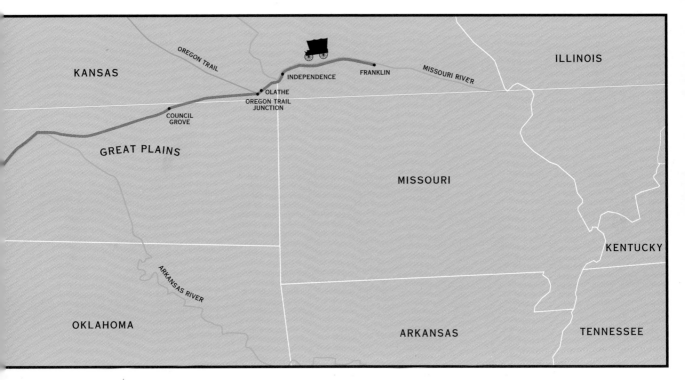

One hundred miles (161 km) beyond Council Grove, the tall grass of the prairies turned into the short grass of the Plains. The land was full of buffalo and antelope. These animals fed the Plains Indians and supplied them with almost everything they needed to live.

Like the Indians, traders on the trail hunted

buffalo and antelope. But many traders killed more buffalo than they needed for food. Soon the Plains were littered with bones and rotting carcasses. The Plains Indians were angered by this and began to attack the wagon trains.

The Plains Indians hunted buffalo for more than food. A buffalo's hide, hair, tail, hooves, bones, and fat were used in the Indians' everyday lives.

The Plains presented another problem for the traders: The short grass made it more difficult for the pack animals to graze. They had to be allowed to roam farther to find food. Yet letting them roam too far from the wagons was dangerous because they might be stolen by the

Indians attacked wagon trains in an attempt to stop traders and trappers from killing the buffalo.

Indians. As a result, traders learned to circle their wagons at night for protection and to take turns standing guard against attack.

The next landmark along the trail was the Arkansas River. It was the mid-point of the journey between Council Grove and Santa Fe. Here, traders used to sing a simple song: *The Arkansas, just halfway/From the States to Santa Fe.*

William Becknell continued across Kansas, following the Arkansas River, and into Colorado before he turned south at the foothills of the Rocky Mountains. He followed the Purgatoire River, which brought him to Raton Pass—a rock-filled mountain crossing where the men had to clear paths for the pack animals. From Raton Pass, the trail went south, passing the sites of the present-day New Mexico towns of Raton, Cimarron, and Las Vegas. Then it swung around the foot of the Sangre de Cristo Mountains to end in Santa Fe.

A present-day view toward Raton Pass

Becknell and his caravan arrive in Santa Fe.

The wagons Becknell used to transport goods were similar to this Conestoga wagon, which was also known as a prairie schooner because it resembled a fast-moving sailing ship.

By the time Becknell arrived in Santa Fe, Old Mexico had successfully gained its independence from Spain (1823). The citizens of Santa Fe were glad to see the traders. The Mexicans needed supplies, so the Americans sold their goods for high prices. Becknell immediately went back to Missouri for more trade goods. According to legend, when Becknell arrived in Franklin, he climbed down from his horse and split open a saddlebag, allowing a shower of silver pieces to fall on the ground. He reported that American traders would now be welcome in Santa Fe.

On his next trip, Becknell wanted to carry more goods than pack animals could manage. He loaded his trade goods into Conestoga-style wagons, sometimes called prairie schooners. (A schooner is a fast sailing ship.) These wagons sat high off the ground with wheels as high as

6 feet (183 cm) tall. They could hold more than two tons of cargo and had curved canvas tops that held goods firmly in place. At least eight draft animals, such as horses, were needed to pull one wagon. Becknell's caravan consisted of twenty-two men and three wagons.

Becknell knew, however, that his wagons could not cross the rocky Raton Pass, so at Cimarron, Kansas, he turned south. Becknell followed what would later become known as the Desert Route (or Dry Route), where people and animals nearly died of thirst on a 50-mile (80-km) stretch where there was no available water. The Desert Route was also beset by Comanche Indians, who attacked wagon trains, killed the men, and took women and children captive.

Lack of water and threat of Comanche attack made travel along the Desert Route difficult and dangerous.

Kit Carson

Charles Bent (middle) and William Bent (bottom) played important roles in the history of the Santa Fe Trail.

Becknell returned to Franklin from his second trip with another large profit. No wonder other traders followed his trail. By the mid-1820s, several caravans were leaving Franklin for Santa Fe each spring.

One man whose name is forever associated with the trail made his first trip in 1826. Kit Carson was sixteen years old that year and was running away from an apprenticeship to a saddlemaker. He became the West's most famous trapper, scout, Indian fighter, and later, Civil War officer.

In the 1820s, the number of traders using the trail was so high that the Mexican government raised tariffs, or taxes, in order to make more money. Casual traders could no longer make a profit. During these years, the Indians also continued to kill traders and to steal horses and mules. U.S. Army soldiers were sent to escort the caravans, but the soldiers could not legally go beyond the Arkansas River. As a result, for a while it looked as if trade on the trail might end.

But when Charles Bent served as captain of his first caravan in 1829, he changed the history of the Santa Fe Trail. Charles and his younger brother, William, were trappers and traders. In 1831, Charles Bent proved the superiority of oxen over mules on the trail. Traders had always used mules because they were faster than oxen and had tougher hooves. But mules were

expensive, and Indians liked to steal them. (An ox was too awkward for an Indian to ride, and its meat was too tough to eat.)

Charles Bent is also credited with the idea of forming a partnership in which one man stayed in Santa Fe to sell goods, while the other man returned to Missouri to collect more goods. Bent went into business with Ceran St. Vrain, a French trapper who lived in Taos, New Mexico, north of Santa Fe. St. Vrain would operate stores in Taos and Santa Fe, while Charles Bent brought goods to those stores from the East. Bent believed he could make two trips each summer if he didn't have to spend time selling the goods himself.

After Charles Bent's journey on the trail, most wagons were pulled by oxen.

William Bent first decided to build a trading post on the Arkansas River for trade with the Plains Indians. He built a simple fort of cottonwood logs at the edge of the mountains, and the Indians brought him buffalo robes that they traded for knives, pots, and lead. In 1832, when Charles arrived with goods to be traded in Santa Fe, William suggested leaving some of them at the fort to trade with the Indians. Charles believed trading with the Indians was dangerous, but he allowed William to persuade him.

Taking goods to and from the fort meant that the caravan would have to cross Raton Pass, where years earlier Becknell had decided wagons could not go. The Bents chopped out a passage by using long, wooden poles to move boulders and shovels to level dirt until they made a path wide enough for the oxen and the wagons.

A present-day view of the interior of Bent's Old Fort, in Colorado

William Bent's trading fort proved so successful that Charles Bent and Ceran St. Vrain decided to build the largest trading post in the American West. Construction began in 1833. Bent's Old Fort, as it is known today, may be the single most important landmark on the Santa Fe Trail. Adobe walls that were 14 feet (4 meters) thick surrounded an area the size of a football field (120 yards, or 110 m). High towers had small slits for riflemen to defend the fort against attack. There was a watchtower where a man with a telescope could stand guard. A bell tower announced meals. The corral held three hundred to four hundred horses, and the fort housed as many as one hundred people.

Many famous people in the history of the American West stopped at Bent's Old Fort, including Kit Carson. Another, Josiah Gregg, made the first of six trips on the trail in 1831 and may have stopped there. Gregg's account of his experiences, *Commerce of the Prairies,* was published in 1844 and is still considered the best firsthand account of life on the Santa Fe Trail.

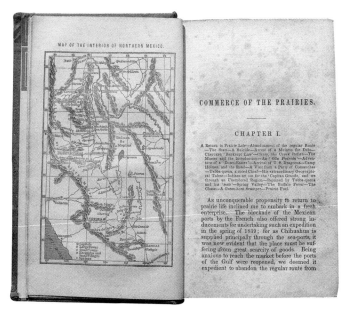

Two pages from Josiah Gregg's book, Commerce of the Prairies

Susan Magoffin

There were not many women on the trail, but Susan Magoffin is remembered for the detailed journal she kept while staying briefly at Bent's Old Fort. Susan was one of the first white women to cross the trail. As an eighteen-year-old bride, Susan traveled with her husband on the trail during their honeymoon in 1846. Susan recorded that she lived comfortably and ate well—one meal consisted of boiled chicken, soup, rice, wine, and gooseberry tart. But she also recorded such hardships as a downpour and flood that left her bed a "floating pond." She suffered a miscarriage on the trip, probably as a result of being thrown from her wagon when it broke loose while descending the steep bank of a creek. Susan recovered at Bent's Old Fort, but her health was frail after that. She died several years later, in 1855.

Texas, which had been controlled by Old Mexico, gained its independence in 1836. As a new republic, Texas claimed land that included Santa Fe and most of New Mexico. This land was west of the boundaries of the Louisiana Purchase, so the Mexican government refused to recognize the claim. In 1841, Texas sent 275 volunteer soldiers to capture Santa Fe, but the mission was poorly planned. The Santa Fe Trail survived the Texans' "invasion" untouched.

In May 1846, when the United States and Old Mexico went to war, Santa Fe became even more important. The trail was closed because of the fighting and the price of goods went higher than ever. By August, General Stephen Watts Kearny took possession of Santa Fe. Shortly after, believing New Mexico safely secured for the United States, Kearny marched his army out of Santa Fe. He appointed Charles Bent as governor.

Towns left without military protection were open to rebellion against the United States. Late in 1846, Charles Bent received news of a con-spiracy against the Americans. Bent was able to stop the rebellion. But in January 1847, when he went to visit his family in Taos, he was assassi-nated by a mob of Mexicans and Indians. Charles appeared, unarmed, at his door to confront the mob. Although he was killed, it may have been his personal bravery that saved his family. Nearly every other American in Taos was killed.

Word of the rebellion reached Santa Fe, where there was a small army detachment. Ceran St. Vrain gathered merchants and trappers to support the soldiers, and the small force went north to meet the rebels. The Americans defeated the rebels, Old Mexico lost the war, and the Southwest became United States territory.

Kearny and his soldiers took control of Santa Fe without a shot being fired.

The 1840s were a time of increasing discontent for the Plains Indians along the trail. The Americans were killing their buffalo herds, cutting down the trees they used for fuel and shelter, and robbing Indian graves for souvenirs. The Pawnee and Arapaho did not attack traders because of their friendship with the Bents, but the Comanche, Kiowa, Ute, and Jicarilla Apache were relentless. Each time an army troop was sent to defeat them, the Indians became more determined to seek revenge. The trail was so dangerous that at times even Kit Carson would not travel it.

The U.S. Army established more forts along the trail to protect traders and settlers. They wanted to buy Bent's Fort, but William Bent burned it

Costumed staff members reenact a trading scene as it would have occurred at Bent's Old Fort.

instead of selling it. Some believe he didn't think the army offered enough money; others suggest he simply couldn't stand to see the fort in the hands of strangers. Today, a reproduction of the fort is maintained by the National Park Service as Bent's Old Fort National Historic Site. It has restored stores, a blacksmith shop, storerooms, a kitchen, and a trading post. The staff wears costumes of the 1830s and 1840s, and travelers get a taste of life on the Santa Fe Trail.

William Bent built Bent's New Fort, about 40 miles (64 km) east of the original fort, but he was not the businessman his brother was and there was no longer much Indian trade. In 1849, the trail again became crowded, this time with forty-niners headed for the California gold rush. Gold seekers used the trail again in 1859, this time hurrying to the strikes and mines in Colorado. But none of it was like the high trade of the days of Bent's Old Fort. In 1860, when the U.S. government built Fort Wise (now called Fort Lyon) near Bent's New Fort, William leased his buildings to the army for storage. The era of the Bents on the Santa Fe Trail was over.

Gold seekers were called "forty-niners," a reference to 1849, the year during which more than 85,000 people went to California to search for gold.

Most people think the Civil War (1861–65) was fought only in eastern and southern states, but Santa Fe and the trail were also threatened by the war. In 1862, Confederate (Southern) troops from Texas invaded New Mexico, seized Santa Fe, and planned to seize the entire Southwest in the name of the Confederacy. Union (Northern) and Confederate troops met on the Santa Fe Trail about 20 miles (32 km) east of Santa Fe at a place known as Pigeon's Ranch. In a six-hour fight now known as the Battle of Glorieta Pass, the Confederates were defeated and New Mexico stayed in the Union.

Glorieta Pass, as it appears today, with the Sangre de Cristo Mountains of northern New Mexico in the background

26

The railroad was gradually moving across the country in the 1860s and 1870s, but traders on the Santa Fe Trail still had to coax oxen across Raton Pass. In those days, most caravans chose the Mountain Route instead of the thirst-building Desert Route. In 1865, at the end of the Civil War, a man known as "Uncle Dick" Wootten blasted rocks, cut away hillsides, and built a toll road across the pass. It was, for its day, a marvelous feat of engineering. At the summit, he built a toll house where he collected fees from travelers. Today, a smooth four-lane highway crosses the pass, but travelers can still see traces of Uncle Dick's toll road.

The railroads brought rapid and permanent change to the West. The land filled with people, and new towns appeared almost overnight along the railroad tracks. The Atchison, Topeka & Santa Fe Railroad moved west on a path that was south of the Santa Fe Trail, but generally paralleled it. A town would be the end-of-the-line, or as far as the train could go, while more railroad tracks were being built farther west. Goods would be shipped by rail to the end-of-the-line town and then taken down the rest of the trail in wagons. Each new end-of-the-line town meant that the towns behind it lost the trade business because the goods sped through town on a train. Many end-of-the-line towns disappeared when the railroad moved beyond them.

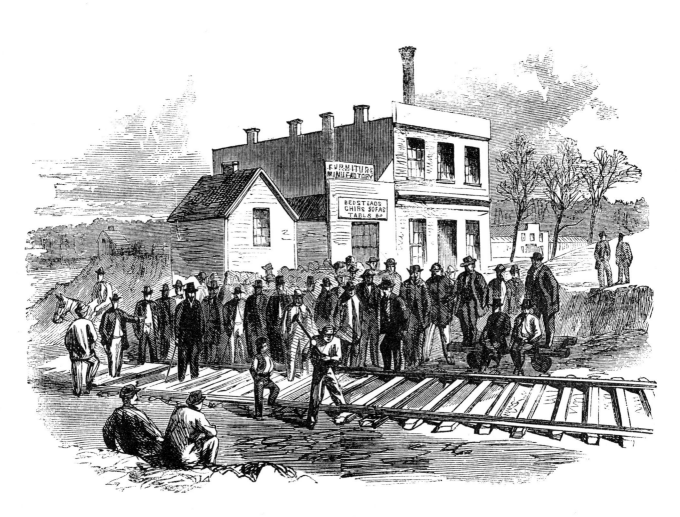

The railroad made travel, transportation, and settlement in the West quicker and easier.

Santa Fe became the end-of-the-line in 1879. The headline in the *New Mexican* newspaper read, "The old Santa Fe Trail Passes into Oblivion."

Today, a granite marker on the Plaza in Santa Fe proclaims the official end of the trail. The Santa Fe Trail had been in use for almost sixty years, and had brought the Southwest into the United States. It remains an important part of U.S. history.

THIS STONE
MARKS
THE

COLORADO

KANSAS

OKLA.

END
OF
THE
SANTA FE
TRAIL
1822 — 1879

TEXAS

ERECTED BY THE
DAUGHTERS OF THE
AMERICAN REVOLUTION
AND THE TERRITORY OF
NEW MEXICO
1910

The marker that commemorates the end of the Santa Fe Trail

GLOSSARY

adobe – traditional southwestern bricks made of water, clay, and straw

apprentice – someone who learns a trade or craft by working with a skilled person

barter – to trade in an exchange of goods rather than for money

caravan – group of people or vehicles traveling together

civilian – person who does not serve in the military

forty-niners – people who rushed to California in 1849 following the discovery of gold

keelboat – shallow boat for carrying freight on rivers

oblivion – the condition of being forgotten or unknown

plaza – open area, near large buildings, that often has walkways, trees, shrubs, and places to sit

province – a district or a region of some countries; for example, Canada is made up of provinces

rendezvous – meeting place

republic – form of government in which the people elect representatives who manage the government

saddlebag – covered pouch that is laid across the back of a horse behind the saddle

toll road – road or highway that requires the payment of a tax in order to travel on it

caravan

forty-niners

TIMELINE

1806
1807 } Zebulon Pike's expedition to Santa Fe

1822 Santa Fe Trail opens; Franklin, Missouri, is trail's starting point

1826 Kit Carson makes his first trip on the trail

1828

Franklin, Missouri, washed away by floods; Independence, Missouri, becomes new starting point

1831 Charles Bent proves oxen superior on trail

1833 Construction of Bent's Old Fort begins

1836 Texas revolts against Mexico

1841 The Texas–Santa Fe Expedition

1846 Mexican–American War

1847

Forty-niners fill trail; William Bent burns down Bent's Fort **1849**

Gold seekers headed for Rockies fill trail **1859**

Confederates defeated at Glorieta Pass **1862**

Uncle Dick's toll road opens **1865**

Charles Bent killed; Susan Magoffin travels Santa Fe Trail

Railroad reaches Santa Fe; **1879** Santa Fe Trail closes

1987 Santa Fe National Historic Trail established

INDEX (*Boldface* page numbers indicate illustrations.)

PHOTO CREDITS

Photographs ©: Archive Photos: 6; Bruce Hucko: 5, 16 bottom, 24; Colorado Historical Society: 18 bottom, 22, 31 right; Corbis-Bettmann: 7, 18 top; Denver Public Library, Western History Department: 18 center; North Wind Picture Archives: 3, 8, 10, 28, 29, 31 bottom left; Reinhard Brucker: 9, 15, 20, 26; Stock Montage, Inc.: 14 bottom (The Newberry Library), 14 top, 16 top, 21, 23, 25, 30 bottom; Superstock, Inc.: 1, 2, 17, 19, 30 top; TJS Design: 4, 12, 13; UPI/Corbis-Bettmann: cover.

ABOUT THE AUTHOR

Judy Alter was born in Chicago but has lived in Texas for thirty years. She is the mother of four grown children and is currently responsible for two large dogs and two cats. Now living in Fort Worth, she is the director of Texas Christian University Press. A novelist and children's author, Ms. Alter is a two-time winner of the Western Heritage (Wrangler) Award from the National Cowboy Hall of Fame.

Ms. Alter is the author of *Sam Houston: A Leader for Texas* and *Cissie Palmer: Putting Wealth to Work* (Community Builders) for Children's Press. She is also the author of *Beauty Pageants, Meet Me at the Fair, Rodeos, Wild West Shows, The Comanches,* and *Women of the Old West* (First Books) for Franklin Watts.